TRIGGER FINGERS

Gerald Arthur Moore

Andrew Lafleche, editor
www.AJLafleche.com

Printed in the United States of America

First Printing: September 2019
Pub House Books
www.PubHouseBooks.com

ISBN-13 978-1-989266-17-5

Grateful acknowledgement is made to the following publications where some of these poems first appeared: The Antigonish Review, Coote's Paradise Writers Anthology, The Nashwaak Review, Off the Coast, Prairie Fire, and Queen's Quarterly.

CONTENTS

Driving Lisa to Drug Rehab

Hatches battened in the head of the gale,
whitecaps slap, the shoreline is a froth.

Lisa's pasted speech is harbour speed
from the junk,

casually mentions that her septum is corroded;
can push her finger all the way through.

Her boyfriend smashed out the storm-door,
There, a mosaic of broken glass glitters

like the glowing Sargasso's highway to the moon.
Dead-eyed corner-boys swim past,

trailer park sharks, dorsal fins, predatorial
turns, always on their chase.

She snorts a Perc, crushed between two quarters,
to smooth the self-loathing of what she has to do,

to quiet the monsters waiting in the depths,
twisting gear, cutting nets, breaking oars.

No markers on the big waters, drifting buoys,
immeasurable borderlines;

blood promises evaporate with her breath,
like tall ships taken by Scylla or Charybdis.

Ninety-six pounds of jagged hipline;
raw nipples, pounded by storms,

anchor tattoos have pinned down her arms,
a hurricane shore littered with wreckage,

the stanchions and beams of her ribcage.
She pulls herself into the car; we cast off,

up the coast with wind in our sails.
When we drift off course, wheels hit rumble-strip,

the rocky promontories that cave-in hulls,
the crashing waves, the noisy gulls.

In the rearview mirror
she fixes one last time;

impossible to know the damage for sure,
or what's under the waterline.

Cité Soleil

For Rich Mears, who survived

Women pass with their wicker crowns
of clean clothes, laughter is a ripe fruit.

Morning inhales, mists evaporate uphill
toward the ramshackle sounds of a beginning.

Dew-wet barefoot children, school bound;
so different from the days after the quake.

That's what I'm thinking, dozing at the wheel
when the passenger door is thrown open.

Lifts up his shirt, shows the taped grip,
the pistol tucked into his waistline

like a vainglorious question mark. A book is
slammed down in my brain. Must have

been a starter pistol; until the blood puddles the seat.
There is a small pea sized hole in the driver's door,

cramping in my leg, and I feel a cloud of shock
darkening like a blanket draped over my head.

The man who drove to the Médecins Sans Frontières
tent didn't know how to drive standard.

Later, I called my phone and spoke to the shooter.
He seemed genuinely relieved that I was alive

and promised to throw the twenty-two
into the Artibonite River,

where the queens of Haiti
are doing their laundry.

Saugeen Arrowhead

The first one I found while
fishing for wood turtles in a watering
hole; it fought hard, but we tugged
that sacred creature streamside;
always turned toward water;
some type of ancient internal compass,
paddled and hissed, drove its claws
into mud to get back.

There, on an oblique angle, it lay
for centuries in sedimentary strata –
a Saugeen chert, edged like an aspen leaf,
chipped by a perfectionist.
A ferric stained imprint in the clay relief
when it slid out, intact.

I heard the voice, and listened.
Released our turtle –
watched her glide down
to the obfuscation of the warm pool.

Fields of goldenrod – paved over,
cattail edges of winding streams –
gone now.
Marshes drained; woodlands bulldozed;
anaemic tin-trimmed houses, sculpted
cedar hedges, interlocking driveway
patterns slant to ditches,
to mighty cisterns;
water is piped off million-dollar
properties down the escarpment
to Hamilton.

My father says they gutted beauty.
He can't see the irony of the arrowhead
or understand the death of our turtle.
Sometimes I hold the stem, run my
finger across the excurvate blade,
gently on the basal edge, and wait
for her to speak again.

Coyotes

Enticed by fresh afterbirth, they infiltrate the barn,
skitter of claws down the manure chute,

dragged that crying calf from her mother
before it could even stand;

like King David's soldiers skulking into the fortified city
through Hezekiah's cistern,

glinting teeth were smiling swords,
oil-stoned edges, Masonic pledges, unspoken words.

Years ago, a shortcut from the old field cemetery
saw my father cross through tangled overgrowth,

a riot of thorns, erratic hazel scourged;
punctured his palms, speared his side, held his arms,

until he sank to the smooth undulation of a rabbit trail,
crawled out like a soldier through coils of razor wire;

the offended tricksters followed him home that night;
left their scat on his doorstep.

After their threat we kept a lame foal in the barn,
and a good thing too,

the next morning there were seven, laying in defilade
behind a berm, at the bottleneck by the paddock gate;

their knackers yard. Turkey vultures, anticipating the kill,
were already flying in their infinite vortices.

Open Wound

Yellowing apples underneath low branches
fermenting; attracting deer and honeybees,
further down the clear-cut they're burning;
turning orchards to floodplains,
smoking stumps, slow to disintegrate,
hold their heat for days.

In slow pirouettes of smoke – a mule deer.
Something wrong, the way she shuffles
awkward – unnatural.

Circling the cut, inside
shadowed tree line, careful outstep
creeping – I'm quiet. Upwind, but that fire
is going to cancel out my scent.
Drift deeper, then arc back out to the edge
of my imaginary clover leaf, slowly emerge,
keep the morning sun in her eyes.
That's when I see it.

Just above her wet cambered shoulder –
a concave exit wound like a cereal bowl;
writhing worms periodically fall, tapping
leaf litter like heavy raindrops. The smoke,
keeping cluster flies at bay, meat bees
from feasting. Maggots, at least
are cleaning this old gunshot.
She's near the end.

Slowly lifts her head when she hears;
tired glass eyes; I understand.
Unsling;
and curse the motherfuckers
who left us like this.

Loss

The needle on the turntable stuttered
over *vegemite sandwich*
while the headboard tapped
to their alien grunting.
Within the closet, without sightline,
amidst this strange confusing cadence
my cramped annex flashed
with destructive understanding.

Unable to wait any longer;
her shawl over my face
to filter the naphthalene,
plucked my penis and voided,
mostly into a boot, then puddling
around my bare feet, expanding
like Ebola across the laminate.

They were throwing Molotov cocktails
in Northern Ireland, slow march
hard-eyed balaclava funerals.
Iranian hostages; Union Carbide's
gas cloud – innocence culled;
and Ryan White – Michelangelo's AIDS angel,
amputated from school, thrown overboard
like a sacrifice to Neptune. A sea of fear.
Nuclear; Chernobyl's melting core;
mutually assured oblivion, Cold War,
cowering under desks
imagining *The Day After*.

Winter cornstalks, flotsam friendships,
graveyard etchings, the troubled lines
of my father's face, lost marbles,
dull chisels, even my sister's virginity
seemed to be a lesson in the long
agony of subtraction;
and a warning.

Hidden Guns

Guitar plectrums pinched with trigger fingers;
din conversations disguised in the confessional

of a snug while uilleann pipe bellows elbow pump.
Her snake wood tipper's percussive blur

like a Spitfire propeller upon the spine of a goatskin –
the meridian. Airy voiced seraphim armed with black

pint glasses; secrets unfold through fiddle leads.
Gun-metal eyes, backs to walls will deny flanking,

thirsty wooden planking, scraping chair legs above *them*,
hidden under floorboards, tight shrouds – oily rags,

balaclavas and tri-colour flags. Remembered,
yet unmapped, like the unmarked graves

of fingerless informants, sleeping in Belfast hills –
scattered seeds beneath hedgerows.

Talking with Aemon, silver hair, bowed shoulders,
when I'm snatched and pommelled,

barely touch the floor as I'm hauled into the alley
by muscled brawlers, tattooed forearms and fists,

hard-eyed serious, car reverses in a flood,
back passenger door yawning like a snake.

"Did the army send you here to ask us questions?"
I fast talk, try not to piss, knees surrender,

trembling lips claim that I came to see
the volunteer graves in Milltown.

Reading truth in each rapid breath, my chest
is a bodhràn drum; the longest caesura.... of my life.

When they believe, tears come. Unfed, the snake
becomes taillights. They apologize.

Back inside they slide a Guinness;
my wedding ring taps like a cymbal.

Their barman produces a key to the cemetery gate.
The Falls Road is watching, gaunt murals

of hunger strikers peer from corner row houses.
Pass through the arch into a forest of Celtic crosses,

standing sentries, for centuries. A topiary
of stone crucifixions, old bones, murdered martyrs,

bombers and blanket men – Bobby Sands
with his comrades of Long Kesh, The New Republican

Plot; smooth polished markers like night sky waters;
the murky depths of resistance, and violence.

The Berlin Wall

We sipped homemade schnapps
from jam-jars. Hundreds of miles
in bar-cars. Holding hands like cherry stems
through checkpoints and border crossings.
In all the ways that mattered, Karen
stamped my passport. *La petit mort* in
The Zeemanshuis in Antwerp, we whispered
of our relatives killing each other.

Her father's East Berlin defection –
an underwater escape, with a jerry-rigged
hot water bottle breathing-apparatus.
Café patrons in wait; jumped into the Spree River,
a splashing mass, trading hats and kissing,
hidden in numbers like piping plovers pinwheeling.
Aiming down, unable to pick him out, border guards
were already phrasing their excuses for the Stasi.

Waiting to leave Kraków, atop a train platform
to forever, she passed me a graffiti tattooed rock –
about the size of an apple;
her piece of the Berlin Wall.
Karen accepted that weight, bundled in her pack
through our heady days together –
chosen like David's sling-stone,
its killing weight, her story.

Mollie Daniel

On leave, she clenched his dog-tags in her teeth
when they made love; her body was a prayer.

His salvation at Dunkirk was a Padre,
who gave up his seat in a rescue boat,

over the gunnel, waded back to the beachhead
bobbing like a shorebird.

Mollie Daniel, driving diesel on D-day,
towing 400 gallons of holy water.

Greasy tarmac beside the muted planes;
soldiers were shading the back of their hands,

trembling cigarettes, teeth gleamed
like sun-bleached-bones against face-paint,

like the chalk cliffs of Dover paired
with the mudscape of the Channel's low tide.

Fearing capture, they cut their unit flashes off,
the bayoneted bare spots on their shoulders complained silently.

Sutured their badges to her scarf; gifts from boyish ghosts;
the Normandy shoreline accepted their blood sacrifice.

Immigrating to Canada, children in tow, one suitcase;
that olive drab Army scarf was folded like love letters,

hasty goodbyes from nameless strangers, faded emblems,
her talisman, drawn together onto the felt landscape of her youth.

That afternoon in London, his dog-tags in her teeth
when they made love; her body a prayer.

Mimesis

Sleepy plywood eyelids
of frowning row houses.

A peal of church bells plays The Westminster –
La di da-da, La di da-da.

There she is again, a soup-spill,
cigarette-ash psoriasis,

carries that naked doll,
her plastic effigy, an albatross;

Child Protective Services peeled her fingers
off the doorframe decades ago.

Stovetop ball-hat corner boys, dial-a-dopers,
fentanyl werewolves, hair-trigger stare, pit bull terriers.

A kid in my wife's class says, "Momma works
on Waterloo Street,"

her emaciated legs have the best veins
for shooting-up,

barefoot in cowboy boots, Johns order her to shower
before they start.

These leaning houses need cleaning ladies;
the city's *priority tenements* are distortion mirrors,

blinds pulled on shuttered lives, Christ,
must mean more than Sunday tithes.

History of the Monad

For Greg, Michelle, and William

Dull wire-rim eye glasses in a picture frame:

The first time Greg saw his wife, he was wearing
someone else's Bolshevik spectacles,
large wire ovals; Trotsky would have worn them,
they were in the style of revolutionaries.

He borrowed them for a moment,
to be able to see the Eiffel Tower.
Through those lenses she appeared;
emerging like an anthem of truth or a raised fist
and declared the world a better place.

That's it. That's how he saw his Beatrice for the first
time – through a pair of borrowed lenses.
She wasn't atop a steel blue mountain – robe billowing,
or unfurling a tri-colour banner, rather,
she was in the contemplative, looking Heavenward.

The mother of his future child,
at the base, staring up into the omphalos of the truss,
shielding her eyes from the glare of progress's arcing
wrought iron triumph.

Their eyes met in recognition and laughing wonderment
in the great monadology of time and space,
where they oscillated and vibrated in tandem
exulting the most optimistic revolutionary notion – that of
romance, the great climb towards the poetic zenith
of union, into the spire of longing, toward a lifetime
of tomorrows together, like two lenses,
bound in a wire frame.

J is my origin story

Like a shorebird with a mussel shell,
in a way that happens in high school;

before a violent drop to breakwater rocks,
the soft exposure of flesh, harvesting of meat.

Secret spies, slipping into equipment room solitude
behind a blooming bin of lacrosse sticks,

the echo drum-percussion of basketballs,
a squeaking myriad of stops and starts.

Through that wardrobe you took me to Narnia's
limitless wonder, on bald tires over highway miles

that summer. One night, pulled over by the OPP speeding;
I was wearing a Grateful Dead tie-dye t-shirt, you were topless,

arms folded in faux modestly. He offered the citation;
a bravo-smile underling his moustache.

Spent a patient afternoon drinking longnecks
and scarifying my back with the letter J, in hickeys.

Now, thumb smudged in a yearbook, you are reclining
across the tank of a motorcycle like a half note rest,

the caesura of our lives, where we paused together,
rolled down backroads, stoned inside stadiums,

skipped stones on the Great Lakes, skipped classes,
found the corners of cornfields, you were bread, and I, molasses.

Even then, the cows were already laying down in the fields, dark clouds calling from the distance.

Jerusalem's Ridge 1996: Canadian Forces Base Gagetown

Last light was an immolation,
the sky looked like well-worn jeans.

.50 cal tracer rounds ricochet upward
like falling stars in reverse.
Blackout road-move, Bombardier Darcy
driving our Iltis, following a glow-stick
taped to a Howitzer barrel,
and a second fixed to its shield – for depth.
Gun tractor drivers wore all the NVGs,
leaving us one pair short.
We adapted.

About an hour later – tumbling
end-over-end like a midway ride.
My rifle, named Lizzie Borden,
had been sleeping on the passenger mirror,
hit terra firma, bounced back into the jeep
– then went berserk.

Lizzie Borden became a pinball that was
strangely attracted to Darcy.
RSM Andrews, who had been directly
behind me, was now in the front with us.
Wheels spinning like vinyl records when
our jeep came to a violent halt on roll bars;
the petrol cap had gone AWOL.
Darcy was cursing the Army
like a mortally wounded Mercutio; some
of his face was hanging from Lizzie's front sight
like a dry-cleaning tag. The RSM,

stoic as a Swiss Guardsman,
smirking with an axe, in a torrent felled a tree,
limbed it and levered the jeep upright.

First light was an immolation,
the sky – well-worn jeans.

Viking Pinecone

In the Archaeology News I'm astonished that
scientists have unearthed a well-preserved
piece of Ninth-Century Viking poop.
Hearty, as you might expect from a Viking.
I show the picture to my three-year-old son.
He's recently taken to calling his solid waste, pinecones.

"That's a pinecone!" He declares in amazement,
perhaps wondering why, "A great big pinecone!"
I tell him it's from a Ninth-Century Viking.
He says, "It's a great big Ninth-Century Viking pinecone."
And I think, one day, he could be excavating a square;
shaving at a layer like Kathleen Kenyon.
Studying stratigraphy, dusting with a small brush
for potsherds, troweling, unearthing coprolites,
to realize our bleak metaphysical hollow;

we are all destined for the same ossuary, desiccating
in the bone box of time after our poem is recited
– for a brief reprieve from the contingent;
offering us something we don't have
in life – a beginning and an end.

Haitian Rice Harvest

Rocks anchor the edges of repurposed blue tarps
with their drumlins of rice drying in the sun;

shovelled with banana palm trays, swirled and tossed
into the air as if they were panning for gold,

the chaff flitters away on the hot breath of afternoon.
Barfoot children walk through harvest mounds

the same way Canadian kids kick
Autumn leaves.

Borel's church school is having its corrugated roof repaired;
rubber cuttings from truck tires are melted in tin cans,

the toxic tar painted into newly sanded metal undulations,
patching rusty lesions that have metastasized

before the wet weather comes. The rice and roof a priority;
this harvest shakes hands with hurricane season.

Days after the earthquake, in a second-floor classroom,
children were playing a game where they stomped

and clapped, imitating a thunderstorm.
Students below fled from windows,

weeping at the memory of shattered amputations,
cinderblock aftershocks, clearing rubble bare-handed.

The youngest kids won't look me in the eye; leftovers
from centuries of stolen sugarcane?

Their parents grip my hand and peer deeply, antimetabole,
perhaps I represent to them what they represent to me.

Cholera is a new ligature, creeping up streams
and rivers, while foreign bags of stars and stripes

sell at every market
twenty percent cheaper than their own rice.

To LGen. Romeo Dallaire

*after "We're Hardcore" by Gord Downie

Dallaire, you've tumbled into this Divine Comedy
with no canto for genocide. Your *contrapasso* is that
of the soothsayers, who walk forever with their
heads on backward.

The metallic scrape of a machete over stone, dragged
lazily against the road, *analepsis* to bloating bodies
pulsing in the tidewater's froth, floating manikins –
like naked Christian statuary bobbing in rivers of blood –
blood muzzled dogs, that unmistakable smell, the
meeting of *Interahamwe* leaders, their emotionless abyss,
the neutral birdsong at daybreak.

Floating above the narthex of Nyarubuye sanctuary –
Christ with his arms out, ignored
as they pried the metal doors, threw their grenades,
surged through with spears on their mad purge.
School uniforms, folded on dovetail pews
in this public mausoleum. Their dry bones
sorted and stacked.

When radio RTLM cackled with Devilish mirth,
the voices of the world were silent. Somehow you stayed
and bore witness; defended the stadiums with soldiers armed
with clipboards.

Mbaye Diagne is one who floats – like that Jesus
above the entrance in Nyarubuye. He could
turn a righteous smile on drunk murderers –
transcend the meanest checkpoints, past thirsting

axes and twisting drills, saving Tutsis by the score;
he was hardcore. Until a mortar attack on a bridge
tore him open like a martyred saint. Without body bags,
you wrapped him in a UN flag and sent him home
to Senegal.

Then the extremists put out a reward for your head;
with cavalier confidence, you let on you were deeply offended;
thought you should be going for more. You're hardcore.
You're hardcore.

Coup de Grâce At The Quinte Hotel

Two sensitive poets tangled in bouquets;
at our Quinte Hotel, Main Street, Moncton.

Al Purdy's blooms appear in our beer,
yellow flowers collar each pour;

they shoot, bud, develop, explode open
in their splendor, then wilt, and die.

We've been reading our verse to each
other; the bartender seems like a

sensitive woman too. She's been checking
us out, with interest.

"Would you like anything else?" Petrarch's
Laura, standing behind the bar,

separated by a causeway of brass and oak;
her hand on her hip, and for some

reason I'm reminded of Eden and the
temptations of quintessential humanity;

when I burst out like Odysseus from the
mouth of our ruse,

with heroic phrasing, so that she would lay
down at the altar of the written word,

"I'd like to be thinner, more handsome, and a
better dancer. Do you have that here?"

It was Shakespearean, contre-blason, with the
stubble of Irving Layton's ridiculous impulsivity.

"Yes, we have that here," she said calmly,
"but I'd have to drink it."

Alec

When Alec's pick-up crunched our lane,
the whiskey was eclipsed by the crock

of pickled pears. He was a stippled
old drunk that smelled like gin-piss;

who, on my eighth Halloween, dropped
a bottle of beer in my pillow case.

Collins Hotel regulars called him a character;
he prophesied like Amos from a barstool,

his children waiting outside for hours.
My father recognized the dark lonely distances

he chose; the empty dreams tossed
from a driver's window,

duds that thumped ditches, brittle glass
offerings that glitter before headlights.

His wife finally left after their kids
emigrated to the edges,

East to Halifax and West to Vancouver,
like bookends.

One lean autumn, Dad bought
Alec's old chesterfield, and paid too much.

Mother brooded for a week, then said,
"You know he just drank it."

Found him beat-to-shit out by The Reserve;
his burnt skeletal truck torched in a cornfield;

boot-marks on his forehead, a broken crown,
one eye pendulous from its socket;

reminded me of a tiny naked bird,
excommunicated from the nest.

Running from Johnny Law

Sulphur Springs was an old friend;
each handhold of that road, known,

with her slalom run of knotted turns,
every footpath and fence, familiar.

Reckless teenage speed,
crested over one hill past an OPP;

flew – literally – none of the
wheels were touching.

Cruiser lights spun-on like fireworks in the rearview.
Hammered the gas-pedal like I was stepping on a shovel,

perhaps the most impetuous decision of my life.
Tapped off the headlights and drove;

taillights fading, wheels squealing protestations
with each turn, tailgate sparks against the inverse slope;

cascade of stars, a waxing gibbous moon
dangling like a plump peach on a low branch,

mileage clicking fast, past St. Andrews cemetery;
hit Wilson Street and let 'er rip,

full tilt, gear-shift smacking in its skirt,
engine winding up; jumped curbstones

behind Glendale Motors, bashed through a hedgerow
across a yard, skidded home under the black chestnut.

Shut it down; the red hot block twitching
as she rested in the dew of fresh cut lawn;

fragrant lilacs and mown grass;
soon crickets resumed their choir song,

until sirens came. One, two, three – their
voices rising then falling, fading, toward the QEW.

Closed the truck door. Hot metallic clicks,
six-cylinders complained of being driven too hard.

The single glowing ember of my father's cigarette
on the back veranda.

ABOUT THE AUTHOR

GERALD ARTHUR (ART) MOORE is an adventurer, part-time university lecturer, high school teacher, and a rugby coach living in Moncton, New Brunswick, Canada. NON-Publishing released his first book of poetry *Shatter the Glass, Shards of Flame* in 2018. His work has appeared in *Queen's Quarterly, Vallum, The Antigonish Review, The Nashwaak Review, The Dalhousie Review, Qwerty, Off the Coast, Prairie Fire, Boston Poetry Magazine,* and *Quills.* Moore is also a playwright, most recently of *Just Another School Shooting* (Heartland Plays Inc.) Moore concludes each class with the mantra, "Be good, don't steal anything, come back to me sober, and girls remember, boys lie."

www.ingramcontent.com/pod-product-compliance
Lightning Source LLC
Chambersburg PA
CBHW021946040426
42448CB00008B/1258